I0823251

INTO THE UNKNOWN

THE LOCH NESS MONSTER

Kevin Cunningham

Mitchell Lane
PUBLISHERS

Mitchell Lane
PUBLISHERS

mitchelllanepub.com

2001 SW 31st Avenue
Hallandale, FL 33009

First Edition, 2026.
Author: Kevin Cunningham
Designer: Ed Morgan
Editor: Morgan Brody

Series: Into the Unknown
Title: The Loch Ness Monster

Library bound ISBN: 979-8-89260-737-7
eBook ISBN: 979-8-89260-742-1

Photo credits: cover, p. 2, 3, 5, 11, 21, 23, 25, 27 Shutterstock; p. 4 , 32 freepik.com; p. 7, 9, 12, 13 wikimedia; p. 15, 17, 19 Alamy

CONTENTS

CHAPTER ONE

MYSTERIOUS WATERS

Urquhard Castle overlooks Loch Ness in Scotland.

George Spicer and his wife took a drive. The government had built a new road nearby. The road passed Loch Ness, a lake in Scotland.

A shocking sight awaited the Spicers. A giant long-necked animal crossed the road. George Spicer said the creature was 25 feet (7.6 meters) long and 4 feet (1.21 meters) high.

He sped up to get closer. But the whale-shaped animal slid into the water.

“I am willing to take any oath that we saw this Loch Ness beast,” George Spicer told a newspaper.

CHAPTER ONE

The newspaper printed a story. An editor described the creature as a monster. Loch Ness Monster **mania** soon swept Great Britain. Reporters hurried to the loch. Boy scouts and hunters joined the search. Small boats dotted the water's surface.

The excitement increased later in the year. Hugh Gray took a walk around the loch. A dark shape stirred the water. Gray took a photo. The picture turned out blurry. But the newspapers printed it. Some people saw a monster in the image.

Loch Ness and the monstrous **Nessie** became world famous. Tourists have flocked to the area ever since. By 2023, 1,155 people said they had seen the creature.

The Loch Ness Monster gets most of the attention. But people around the world have reported lake monsters. In some cases, the sightings go back a long time.

FAST FACT

Loch Ness is 21 miles (35 kilometers) long. It holds the most water of any lake in Great Britain.

CHAPTER TWO

AROUND THE WORLD

Roy Mackal studied biology at the University of Chicago before becoming interested in lake monsters.

Roy Mackal visited Loch Ness in 1965. He heard stories. The scientist began to study lake monsters.

Folklore said a long-necked beast roamed Central Africa. Mackal journeyed to the Republic of the Congo. The Lingala people called the monster *mokele-mbembe*. The name meant "one who stops the flow of rivers." Some witnesses said it roared.

FAST FACT

Many rivers form the Congo River basin. These waterways flow into the Congo. The basin touches 7 countries: Angola, Cameroon, the Central African Republic, the Democratic Republic of the Congo, the Republic of the Congo, Tanzania, and Zambia.

Mackal failed to find the mokele-mbembe. But his **expedition** made the creature famous.

In Turkey, Lake Van may cover an ancient castle. Divers rediscovered the ruins in 2017. But they had been searching for *Vana Ichi hresh*, the Lake Van monster.

Argentina's lake monster lives in Nahuel Huapi Lake. The Tehuelche people told stories of the creature. In 1922, a gold miner saw *Nahuelito*. He called it a "long-neck, swan-headed creature." Modern-day tourists visit the lake town of Bariloche, Argentina. They hope to see the monster.

Lake Van in eastern Turkey is the country's largest lake.

CHAPTER TWO

Lake Champlain sits between New York and Vermont. The indigenous Abenaki warned French explorers about a water **serpent**. Samuel Champlain described a monster in 1609. Sightings took place throughout the 1800s. In 1906, sailors said the creature chased their boats. New sightings take place each year. Locals nicknamed the monster *Champ*.

A 2012 viral video showed a creature snaking through Lake Lagarfljót in Iceland. Sightings of the *Lagarfljót Worm* began in the 1300s.

FAST FACT

The Champ legend inspired the name of a college league baseball team. The Vermont Lake Monsters played in Burlington, Vermont.

This 1977 photo supposedly showed Champ swimming in Lake Champlain.

CHAPTER THREE

NESSIE

The famous "surgeon's photograph" sparked Nessie mania in 1934.

Many people see the Loch Ness monster by accident.

R. Kenneth Wilson took a photo in 1934. The creature looked like a dinosaur. It held its head and neck above the water. People believed Wilson. He was a physician. No one thought a doctor would take part in a **hoax**. The "surgeon's photograph." became the best-known image of Nessie.

CHAPTER THREE

Arthur Grant was on his motorcycle. He surprised the creature. *The New York Times* reported: "The object, taking fright, made two great bounds, crossed the road, and plunged into the loch."

"It was a mixture of browns, greens, sludgy sort of colors," Val Moffat said to PBS.org. "I nearly drove off the road."

Other investigators look for the monster on purpose.

Sir Edward Mountain organized searchers in 1934. Mountain's team reported 21 creature sightings.

FAST FACT

Dinosaurs called plesiosaurs were up to 43 ft (13.1 m) long. Their long necks made up half their body length. Some people suggest monsters like Nessie and the mokele-mbembe might be plesiosaurs. But scientists believe the animals died out with the rest of the large dinosaurs 65 million years ago.

CHAPTER THREE

Robert Rines searched Loch Ness for 25 years. He used underwater cameras. One took a surprising picture in 1972. Rines claimed the image showed a giant flipper.

In 2023, Loch Ness Exploration and the Loch Ness Centre invited volunteers to the lake. Underwater microphones listened. Drones buzzed overhead. People watched through binoculars.

Organizers claimed the event found clues. They reported, "four mysterious and previously unheard loud noises" and a "giant shadow."

Environmentalist Sir Peter Scott (left) with Robert Rines.

FAST FACT

Robert Rines trained dolphins to carry cameras in Loch Ness. He invented gear that improved radar and **sonar**. At age 11, he played violin with Albert Einstein. He used his musical skills to write music for Broadway shows.

CHAPTER FOUR

BENEATH THE SURFACE

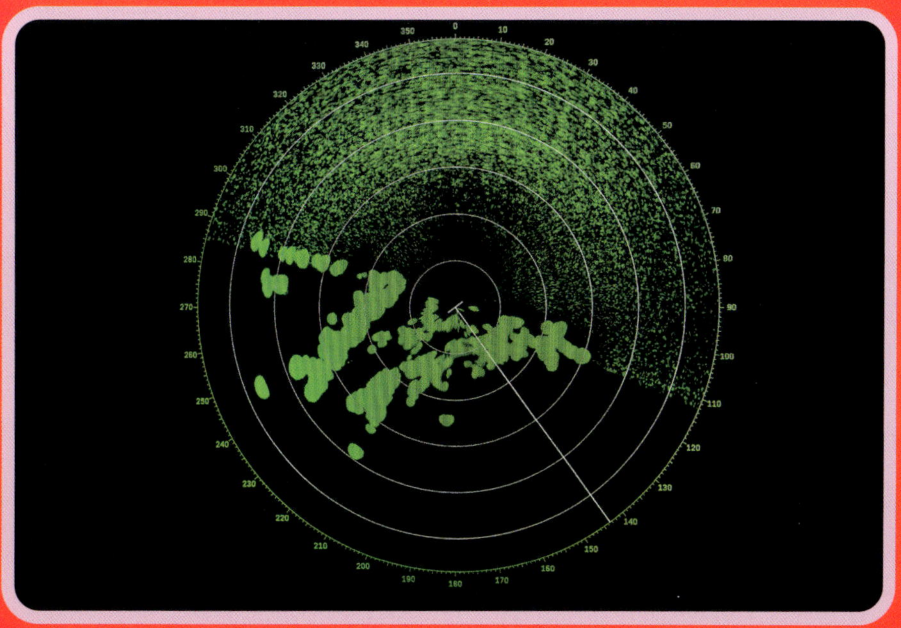

Scientists test ideas. They use the **scientific method**. The process works this way. A scientist makes a prediction. An investigation gathers evidence. Does the evidence support the prediction or not? A scientist wants to answer that question.

We use sonar technology to scan deep water. Sonar's sound waves can find objects or movement. In 2003, researchers used 600 sonar beams to search Loch Ness. "We saw no signs of any large living animal," researcher Ian Florence told bbc.com.

CHAPTER FOUR

Evidence of the Loch Ness Monster often relies on a witness. But people may see what they expect to see. Experts call it expectant attention. The 2003 sonar team ran an experiment. They raised a fence post out of the water. Some onlookers claimed it was a monster's head.

Neil Gemmell tested an idea in 2018. Gemmell studies environmental DNA (called eDNA). Animals' bodies shed eDNA in hair, skin, and other waste products.

Gemmell's team collected eDNA. Their tests showed what lived in the loch.

The eDNA showed no sign of a giant monster. But eels lived all over Loch Ness. Gemmel told Sciencefocus.com, "Therefore we can't discount the possibility that what people see and believe is the Loch Ness Monster might be a giant eel."

FAST FACT

Studies show people often misremember. Marte Otten studies memory. She described what happens. “You saw it correctly,” she said, “but as soon as you commit it to memory stuff starts going wrong.”

CHAPTER FIVE

HISTORY OF HOAXES

Hoaxers goof on the Loch Ness Monster. The tricks go back almost 100 years.

A hoaxer's **motive** can be many things.

The "surgeon's photograph" was about getting even. A newspaper embarrassed Marmaduke Wetherell. He had tried an earlier Loch Ness hoax. The paper caught him.

Wetherell had another idea. His son's stepbrother Christian built a model. The model was a monster head glued to a toy submarine. R. Kenneth Wilson snapped the picture as a joke. Christian described the hoax in 1994. No one expected the false monster to succeed in such a big way.

CHAPTER FIVE

Hoaxers may be playing a practical joke. Sometimes the joker also has a purpose.

George Edwards photographed Nessie in 2011. Monster hunters called it the best-ever shot of the creature. It was not. Edwards operated a tourist boat on Loch Ness. He faked the image to bring more visitors to Loch Ness.

Skeptics point to the research. Scientists have looked and looked, they say. There is no sign of a monster. Believers in Nessie have their own ideas. They argue that scientific investigations can and do miss evidence. And would so many eyewitnesses be wrong?

In the meantime, people keep watching the waters of lakes around the world.

FAST FACT

Local people can profit from lake monster tourism. But not everyone believes in the monster. Travel writer Redmond O'Hanlon went to the Republic of the Congo. He was writing a story about the mokele-mbembe. A local man told him that people passed along monster stories "to bring idiots like you here. And make a lot of money."

TIMELINE

565 CE St. Columba records that a water beast lives in Loch Ness

1700s The Abenaki people warn French explorers of a creature in Lake Champlain

1776 Lievain Bonaventure Proyart describes a giant footprint he saw in Central Africa

1933 George Spicer and his wife claim to see a monster in Loch Ness

1934 R. Kenneth Wilson takes the "surgeon's photograph" of Nessie

1980 Roy Mackal's expedition searches for the mokele-mbembe

1994 Alastair Boyd shows the "surgeon's photograph" was a hoax

2003 Sonar fails to find the Loch Ness Monster

2018 Neil Gemmell looks at eDNA in Loch Ness

GLOSSARY

expedition (ek-speh-DISH-en)
A journey with a specific purpose

folklore (FOK-lor)
The beliefs and stories of a group or community of people

hoax (HOKS)
A fake or trick used to deceive others

mania (MAY-nee-a)
A feeling of extreme excitement

motive (MO-tiv)
The reason for doing something

Nessie (NESS-ee)
The nickname for the Loch Ness Monster

scientific method (SI-en-TIF-ik ME-THed)
A list of tasks for testing scientific ideas

serpent (SUR-pent)
A giant snake-like reptile

sonar (SO-nar)
A technology for detecting objects or movement underwater

FACT CHECK

1. **What does sonar use to take underwater images?**

   A. Lasers beams
   B. Sound
   C. X-rays
   D. Infrared

2. **Sightings of Nessie, Nahuelito, and the mokele-mbembe often mention which body part?**

   A. White fur
   B. Two heads
   C. Spikes on the back
   D. A long neck

3. **The monster in the "surgeon's photograph" turned out to be which object?**

   A. The rubber creature used to film a horror movie
   B. A dinosaur called a plesiosaur
   C. A fake head on a toy submarine
   D. Trained otters

4. **Which fact about Loch Ness is true?**

   A. The water never freezes
   B. It's located in Scotland
   C. It holds the most water of any lake in Great Britain
   D. All of the above

Answers: B, D, C, D

FIND OUT MORE

IN PRINT

Harper, Benjamin. *The Secret Life of the Loch Ness Monster*. Captone: North Mankato, MN: 2023.

Korté, Steve. W*hat Do We Know about the Loch Ness Monster?* New York: Penguin Workshop, 2022.

Oachs, Emily Rose. *The Loch Ness Monster*. Bellwether Media: Minnetonka, MN: 2018.

ON THE INTERNET

BBC Scotland. "Searching for Evidence: They Created a Monster." Via YouTube. Video.
www.youtube.com/
watch?v=2cphhC3E_8Q&list=PL5tFdO7wRD
HmG3eHq6wGhNleEKz_AmFTh&index=1

National Geographic. *Drain the Oceans: Uncovering the Secrets of Loch Ness*. Via YouTube. Video.
www.youtube.com/watch?v=tktlgInOAF8

National Geographic. *Plesiosaurs 101*. Via YouTube. Video.
www.youtube.com/watch?v=mkw593Qa19U

INDEX

About the Author

Kevin Cunningham has written over 120 books on history, medicine, careers, and climate change. He lives near Chicago, Illinois. He likes to imagine that a monster lives in Lake Michigan.